Learning LOL

Welcome to my class on Pronuncations! My name is Professor Charlie, and I am so excited to show you all the fun things my assistant and I have been learning. My assistant is my mom, and she is super helpful! She reads all of the research we do together out loud, takes me for walks when it is time for a break, finds yummy treats for the both of us to share, and also does all the typing since she has fingers and thumbs, and I only have paws, and the most important thing of all, she gives the best belly rubs. My job is to give her fun ideas to look up, to keep her warm with cuddles, and to try not to bark at the mailman. I make no promises about the last one. We make a really great team!

Right after an early morning rain one spring day, the sun came out and warmed everything up, and the afternoon turned into a perfect day. My assistant and I decided to leave the office and enjoy the day. Where we live in Michigan (it is the state that looks like a mitten with the big lakes around it), we don't get a lot of sun during the winter, so when we see the sun shining and a little bit warm, we need to grab our favorite drinks, water for me and coffee for my assistant, and go to the dog park. I love seeing all my pup pals because we always have so much fun chasing each other around, smelling all the new smells since the last time we were here, and running to see who can get to the ball first after one of our humans throws it. I have many pup pals at the park, and we have so much fun together. My favorite game is puppy tag! It is so much fun running around and chasing each other. My pup pal Scarlet is so fast! I know if I keep practicing, I will be just as fast.

When we arrived at the park, my Mom, I mean, my assistant, found a great spot to relax. She took off my leash and took a blanket from her park bag. I helped her lay it on the grass under a tall tree. She sat with her coffee, told me to have fun with my friends, and started reading a book. I ran over to my friends Scarlet, a samoyed; Lily, a golden retriever; Jack, a mini dachshund; Smokey, a corgi; and E, a French bulldog. I was so excited to see everyone! As I was running up, I noticed that there was a

new dog, a Siberian husky I had never met before with my friends. I love meeting new pups! When I reached my friends, I said hi to everyone, then turned and introduced myself to the new dog. "Hi! My name is Charlie. What is your name?" The new dog gave a little wave with his paw and a small smile but didn't answer my question. My friends told me they had been trying to talk to him, but he wouldn't talk to them. I told them he might be a little shy, and maybe after some time getting to know us, he would open up. So I asked if anyone wanted to play tag, and everyone's tail began to wag, even the new dog.

After about thirty minutes of playing and only taking small water breaks, we all lay down, laughing and panting under the shade of the tree, even the new pup. My assistant brought us all bowls of water and a peanut butter dog treat. After a few minutes, I again asked the new pup his name. He looked at me and opened his mouth like he was going to speak but quickly closed it and looked down, embarrassed. Scarlet told him we were all friends now and would like him no matter what. After she said that, we all agreed, wagged our tails, and encouraged him to speak!

The new dog looked up with a small smile and took a deep breath, "My name is Ev–Ev–er-Everest." He quickly looked down and closed his eyes in embarrassment because of how he talked. I walked over to Everest, tilted my head upside down with my eyes crossed, and stuck my tongue out. I told him to open his eyes, and he let out a huge laugh! Afterward, we comforted him and said that we would never make fun of him for how he spoke and that we couldn't wait to return to the park again and play with him. We talked to Everest for about 10 minutes before we all had to go home. During our conversation, he told us he has always had trouble with his "v" sounds, which is unlucky because the letter "v" is in his name. Because of this, he never really liked talking to anyone. Jack told him, you are our friend now and gave him a high five! Everyone else agreed! Everest said he was having trouble finding pronunciation help. Hearing this made me sad, but then, I got a super amazing idea! Maybe my assistant and I could make something for Everest to help him practice. I told him my idea, and his tail wagged so hard that I thought he would fly back to his owner! I told him the next time I came to the park, I would bring some words and

sentences to help him practice. He smiled, thanked me, and told me he was so happy that he had made new friends, and then ran back to his owner. As my assistant and I walked back to the car, I told her about my new friend and my new idea!

When we got home, we got right to work. My assistant and I looked up a lot of words with the letter "v" at the beginning, middle, and end of words and put them into groups where he could practice the sound in different parts of the word. Then we had so much fun writing super silly sentences with these words in them. Each silly sentence makes the speaker slow down and focus on each word. When we were all done with the letter "v," I thought, If my new friend Everest has trouble with a "v" sound, are there other pup pals who have trouble with other sounds? I asked my assistant about this, and she said yes. Some people have trouble with "oo" sounds and "th" sounds. I had no idea so many pup pals had trouble with certain sounds. I sat for a second, a little sad, thinking how Everest felt and knowing that other friends like him were out there. So, I turned to my assistant and asked if we could write some more common sounds pups might have trouble with. Of course, she said yes, and we got right to work!

So we wrote this small book for Everest and for all of you, my new pup pals. After we were done writing this book, my assistant emailed a copy to Everest's mom, and he has been practicing every day. I am meeting him this weekend at the dog park. He can't wait to show me his progress. I hope you enjoy our book, our new pup pal. We will see you for your next lesson!

Tara & Charlie Morrish

Photos by
Scarlet Morrish

Professor Charlie

Smokey

Learninglol.com

Learning LOL

Where learning language online is fun!

We want to thank you, from the bottom of our paws to the tips of our ears, for buying our book! We hope you enjoyed reading it as much as we enjoyed writing and researching it. We are also excited to share that you can join us on our website soon. Here, you can view your favorite topics with videos, maps, pictures, interactive worksheets, and flashcards. To makc cntcring thc classroom easier, scan the QR code, but remember to ask your grown-up before going online. See you there!

Have fun learning online!

Have fun learning with more books!

Learninglol.com

Learning LOL

Where learning language online is fun!

Learning About the Sounds Letters Make!

Table of Contents

Where learning language online is fun!

Learning About the Sounds Letters Make!

Words with the letters "ER"

Where learning language online is fun!

Learning About the Sounds Letters Make!

Learning About the Sounds Letters Make!

Words with the letters "ER"

Words Starting with "ER"

Eric, Erica, Erikson, Erin, Erma, Erroll, error, erase, eraser, erect, erode, errand, erupt

Words with "ER"

Berlin, Bernie, German, Herman, Hermes Laverne, Mercury, Sherman, alert, berry, camera, certain, different, emerge, exert, fern, fierce, funeral, herb, herd, here, interval, mercy, merely, merk, mystery, nerd, nervous, observe, operate, pattern, period, perm, permit, person, reverse, serve, superb, terrace, terrific, terror, their, there, verb, versus, villagers, were, where, zero

Words ending with "ER"

Alexander, Asher, Denver, Harper, Rochester, Roger, Together, Tyler, Vancouver, after, another, appetizer, baker, bewilder, brother, butler, butter, buzzer, chamber, cheer, computer, darker, eager, enter, fever, fiber, finger, fixer, gamer, hardcover, joker, lier, order, otter, over, river, ruler, sister, super, theater, thermometer, thicker, thinker, thinner, thriller, thrower, thunder, tiger, tower, traveler, user, water

Learning About the Sounds Letters Make!

Words with the letters "ER"

"ER" Pronunciation Sentences

1. The baker was bewildered after twelve tigers jumped down the tower and swam over the river to place an order for appetizers.

2. The darker chamber under the tower thrilled Roger until he saw a tiger eating butter because it confused him.

3. The clever carpenter was the fixer of his balder brother's darker chamber.

4. Arthur invited his sister, brother, the tired traveler, and twelve white tigers.

5. The thick tiger had a sister and brother who loved appetizers.

6. Erma had erased Tyler's erupting volcano on the computer.

7. Erroll and his butler went to Berlin to buy some thicker butter, darker water, and a hardcover book from the author, Ashor Tower, "Over Another Bewildered Ruler."

8. Erica was eager to erect a permanent tower with a theater and yummy appetizers from the baker.

9. Harper ordered fewer ferns than Roger, so they worked together.

10. The ruler loved the buzzer to make the villagers erupt with laughter.

Learning About the Sounds Letters Make!

Words with the letters "ER"

"ER" Pronunciation Sentences

11. The gamer had a fever after the butler ordered an appetizer of butter and fiber bread.

12. Over the river was a tower with the tiger's sister Erma inside. The tower was thinner, not thicker, so the tiger entered the tower under the river.

13. Asher, Erroll, Tyler, and Erin went to Denver to cheer up the baker, who, with the butler, needed the appetizers in order.

14. The Erie Canal has brothers, sisters, mothers, and fathers bewildered by the super water.

15. Erikson was a super traveler who entered an adventure over the water.

16. Harper was Rochester's biggest joker, liar, and butterfingers.

17. The water entered the cave and eroded the chamber.

18. Alexander, the ruler of Vancouver, had a perm, and the villagers were eager to see it.

19. Eric had mercy on Roger after his computer fibers were on fire.

20. In the tower with Erica was a tiger from Denver and an otter from Rochester.

Where learning language online is fun!

Learning About the Sounds Letters Make!

Where learning language online is fun!

Learning About the Sounds Letters Make!

Words with the letter "L"

Where learning language online is fun!

Learning About the Sounds Letters Make!

Learning About the Sounds Letters Make!

Words with the letter "L"

Words Starting with "L"

Leo, Lewis, Lily, Linda, Lisa, Logan, Lola, labor, ladder, lady, lamb, lamp, lantern, large, lasagna, laser, last, laugh, laundry, lava, lavish, law, lawn, lay, lazy, leader, leap, leaves, leg, legend, lemonade, leopards, let, lettuce, lice, lick, light, like, lime, limo, lion, lipstick, listen, litter, little, live, lizard, lobster, location, lock, locker, lockup, lollipop, look, lord, loser, loud, low, luck, lumber, lunch, lunchbox, lurk, lute, luxury

Words with "L"

Alex, Elizabeth, Melanie, Melvin, Scarlet, Shelley, adult, alive, apple, below, blazer, blind, block, blood, blue, cable, calm, child, children, clock, cold, decline delay, early, elf, file, flow, glass, gold, golf, health, hole, island, itself, male, mile, place, plate, please, policy, purple, salt, sample, silver, sleep, slow, sly, smile, split, table, truly, twelve, volume, walk, weekly, whole, world, would, yield

Words ending with "L"

Annabell, Carol, Daniel, Hazel, Noel, Shantel, awful, bagel, bill, boil, bowl, capitol, cereal, coal, crawl, doll, duel, eel, equal, evil, fail, final, fool, fuel, girl, global, goal, howl, jewel, label, mail, mammal, marvel, meal, mental, metal, model, motel, mural, novel, oral, oval, pearl, pill, playful, pool, rail, roll, seal, snail, social, soil, soul, swirl, symbol, tool, towel, travel, unequal, yell

Learning About the Sounds Letters Make!

Words with the letter "L"

"L" Pronunciation Sentences

1. Lamb and leopard liked taking a limo to listen to twelve lobsters laughing.

2. Lewis's lunchbox had blue lettuce and a gold lollipop.

3. Lion and lizard saw lava traveling slowly for miles.

4. Daniel licked the lollipop that tasted like leaves and looked like a golf ball.

5. Scarlet did laundry for Hazel, who had silver lipstick on her blazer.

6. Lily went to the pool, and a little eel was listening to loud music.

7. The children lurked near the locker, looking at the lady on the lawn.

8. Please sample the whole apple on the plate on the purple table.

9. Live lobsters use lasers as lanterns as they laugh and lock up the little, loud, leaping lambs.

10. The little loud leaping lambs ate lasagna, lettuce, and licked lemonade while in lock up.

11. Lewis was the leader of the cool global sleep club.

Learning About the Sounds Letters Make!

Words with the letter "L"

"L" Pronunciation Sentences

12. The lavish lady traveled in luxury and ate a large lobster for lunch.

13. Logan emptied the lion's litter weekly behind the lumber place.

14. Lola locked the gold in a metal lunchbox with a whole lollipop.

15. The light blue plate was alive below the rail and looking for an apple.

16. Twelve laughing children listened to the lute and read novels.

17. Daniel was the weekly loser, so the Lord locked him in a block of lasagna.

18. The adult looked at the clock below the hole and smiled because there was no delay.

19. The location the lizard told Scarlet was on a lavish lawn with loud, laughing children and sleeping lambs.

20. The lucky lime lost the race and wouldn't become lemonade.

Learning About the Sounds Letters Make!

Where learning language online is fun!

Learning About the Sounds Letters Make!

Words with the letters "LL"

Where learning language online is fun!

Learning About the Sounds Letters Make!

Learning About the Sounds Letters Make!

Words with the letters "LL"

Words starting with "LL"

Llana, Lloyd, llama, llano

Words with "LL"

Allen, Billy, Collin, Gabriella Kelly, Lillian, Mellissa, Molly, Sally, alligator, allow, ballet, balloon, bellow, billion, bulldog, bullet, bully, cellar, chilly, college, dollar, fallen, fellow, fellow, fully, gallop, gazelle, gorilla, hallway, hello, hilly, jello, jolly, mallet, million, mullet, pillow, pollen, pollute, rally, really, roller, shallow, silly, skillet, smelly, swollen, tally, valley, valley, vanilla, villa, villain, volley, wallet, willow, yellow

Words ending with "LL"

Abdull, Abigall, Annabell, Dell, Kendall, Terrell, all, anthill, bell, bull, call, cell, chill, cowbell, doll, drill, drumroll, drywall, dwell, eyeball, fell, fill, full, goofball, grill, gumball, hill, install, kill, krill, mall, meatball, misspell, molehill, overall, pinball pull, quill, refill, retell, roll, scroll, sell, shall, shell, shrill, skill, skull, small, smell, spell, still, stroll, tall, thrill, troll, unroll, unwell, uphill, wall, waterfall, well, will, yell

Learning About the Sounds Letters Make!

Words with the letters "LL"

"LL" Pronunciation Sentences

1. Billy spent a dollar on a yellow balloon after his meatball fell on an anthill.

2. The smelly cowbell rolled downhill, close to the waterfall.

3. The tall villain strolled down the hallway, looking for the College of Ballet.

4. Abigall ate a billion vanilla jello balls and then bellowed that her belly hurt.

5. Collin's bulldog pulled the pillow into the cellar and said, "Hello."

6. The roller coaster was full of fellas and villains with mullets.

7. Kendall, the jolly galloping alligator, followed the drumroll to the chill molehill.

8. Molly installed an eyeball on the wall to scroll over her spelling.

9. The troll yelled to the gorilla to smell the meatball from the mall.

10. The doll was a tall, chilly ballet bulldog who misspelled "shallow."

11. The valley had a jolly alligator who allowed millions of goofballs to play in jello.

Learning About the Sounds Letters Make!

Words with the letters "LL"

"LL" Pronunciation Sentences

12. Lillian and Kelly used a mallet and a skillet to play volleyball.

13. Abdull refilled the small gumball machine that fell while rolling down the hill.

14. Lloyd filled the cellar with vanilla pillows and chilly yellow gazelles.

15. The drywall was unrolled because the smelly jello was not chilly.

16. The silly gazelles help pollinate the small yellow flowers in the valley.

17. Molly pulled out a skillet and made a vanilla wallet cake.

18. Llana rolls downhill over a molehill and an anthill through the valley into the waterfall.

19. Kelly shall stop the villain Billy by selling his cowbell.

20. Collin was a bully in the college, but Abigall, Dell, and Kendall were smelly goofballs who could spell.

Where learning language online is fun!

Learning About the Sounds Letters Make!

Words with the letters "OO"

Learning About the Sounds Letters Make!

Learning About the Sounds Letters Make!

Words with the letters "OO"

Words Starting with "OO"

Oogy, Ooma, Oona, Oorja, ooze, oocyte, oodles, ooh, oology, oolong, oomiak, oops

Words with "OO"

Brook, Brooklyn, Cooper, Roosevelt, Sookie, Woodrow, baboon, blood, bloom, booger, boot, broom, cocoon, cookie, cooler, doodle, doom, door, drool, flood, floor, food, fool, foot, gloom, good, gooey, goofy, goose, groom, groovy, hood, hoodie, hook, indoor, lagoon, look, lookup, loot, maroon, mood, moon, moose, noon, poodle, poof, pooh, raccoon, reboot, roof, saloon, school, shoot, smooch, smooth, snooze, spooky, spoon, swoon, toon, tooth, troop, unhook, wood, woof, wool, wooly, zoom

Words ending with "OO"

Aboo, Roo, Yazoo, achoo, bamboo, boo, booboo, boohoo, cockapoo, cockatoo, coo, cuckoo, didgeridoo, goo, hullabaloo, igloo, kangaroo, moo, peekaboo, poo, shampoo, shoo, skiddoo, switcheroo, taboo, tattoo, too, voodoo, wahoo, yahoo, zoo

Learning About the Sounds Letters Make!

Words with the letters "OO"

"OO" Pronunciation Sentences

1. The moose drooled as he snoozed on the bamboo floor.

2. Roosevelt was a spooky raccoon who was a groovy oology.

3. Ooma and the poodle were eating gooey cookies.

4. The baboon was in a bad mood after he was fooled by shampoo.

5. Oona had a cockapoo who played the didgeridoo next to the lagoon.

6. Brooklyn said achoo in the igloo while playing peekaboo under the full moon.

7. Roo brought good food to the zoo after he got a tattoo.

8. The raccoon woofed and mooed as he doodled a broom.

9. Yazoo, Brook, and Aboo saw a gloomy goose on the flooded lagoon.

10. There were oodles of poodles eating bamboo and yelling, "Boo!"

11. Oogy was the groovy groom who wore a hoodie with a doodle of a cookie.

12. The cuckoo went to school looking for Brooklyn to give her a smooch.

Learning About the Sounds Letters Make!

Words with the letters "OO"

"OO" Pronunciation Sentences

13. The wool of the raccoon was smoother than the goose who was doing voodoo with a tooth.

14. Noon was when the cockatoo built an igloo and a doomed oomiak.

15. Roosevelt had a bloody booger, which is taboo, and now is on Yahoo.

16. A saloon is cooler to play a groovy didgeridoo than a reboot of spooky moo.

17. The wood door was made from bamboo, which Oona traded a poodle and boot for.

18. A poodle made the shampoo from food from school that oozed and was gooey.

19. The cookie flower bloomed maroon at noon and not under a gloomy moon.

20. Brook had a bloody tooth from a spoon after eating taboo food.

Learning About the Sounds Letters Make!

Where learning language online is fun!

Learning About the Sounds Letters Make!

Words with the letter "T"

Where learning language online is fun!

Learning About the Sounds Letters Make!

Learning About the Sounds Letters Make!

Words with the letter "T"

Words Starting with "T"

Tara, Ted, Theresa, Thomas, Tim, Tony, Tyler, table, take, talk, tan, target, task, tax, teacher, team, technology, telephone, television, thank, their, theory, there, thing, think, thirty, those, thousand, threat, three, through, throw, time, today, together, tomorrow, tool, total, touch, tow, town, trade, tradition, train, training, travel, trial, tried, trip, trouble, true, truly, trumpet, try, tub, tummy turn, twelve, twenty, two

Words with "T"

Courtney, Jonathan, Letty, Otis, Patty, Peter, Stella, Steve, active, after, both, chapter, city, culture, data, date, depth, detail, doctor, duty, earth, enter, item, late, match, nation, onto, operate, other, party, path, photo, picture, pretty, quite, rate, route, safety, site, staff, stage, stand, star, start, state, stay, step, stood, stop, store, story, study, total, update, vital, waste, white, winter, with, write, wrote, youth

Words Ending with "T"

Elliott, Grant, Janet, Matt, Robert, Scarlet, Violet, Wyatt, about, accept, act, ant, at, bat, bought, budget, built, cast, caught, client, coast, correct, count, court, cut, difficult, eight, elephant, event, event, excellent, feet, fight, first, foot, front, giant, great, gut, heart, hut, impact, important, it, least, light, lost, might, must, nest,

Learning About the Sounds Letters Make!

Words with the letter "T"

Words Ending with "T"

next, night, parent, past, pet, plant, point, post, pot, president, print, rest, rest, right, select, sheet, short, start, street, tonight vent, vet, visit, weight, went

"T" Pronunciation Sentences

1. Robert spent most of his time lost with a ghost named Tim and his pet named Grant.

2. The rest I will get most in my nest at night is under my violet sheets.

3. Traveling together, Wyatt and Scarlet went to rest in the best tent, but Wyatt had stinky feet.

4. Thomas had a moat with a goat in a boat with thirty trumpets.

5. Janet fought that giant ghost right in front of the president, Tara, and Grant with sweet treats.

6. I count eight sweet treats the ghost has right in front of his wacky floating whale.

7. Eight great boats went very far over that great moat.

8. The great event for boats was west, not east, but watch out for the feet.

Learning About the Sounds Letters Make!

Words with the letter "T"

"T" Pronunciation Sentences

9. Tim and Tyler took the train through the tunnel to trade telephones with Ted.

10. Violet caught a giant ant and built a perfect nest out of cut ten-foot plants.

11. Together, the team must select a short bat for tonight's important event.

12. The task was truly too difficult for Thomas, but his excellent teacher, Matt, helped.

13. Tony traded two televisions for eight heart-shaped tarts.

14. Theresa is training for the important foot race tomorrow at Grant Park.

15. Scarlet touched the turtle and painted a teal foot and heart on its tummy.

16. I have a great pet tiger named Tim, who I caught in a difficult net.

17. Ted and Matt fought about the client who lost their pet bat right in front of the hut.

18. Three giant goats and eight tiny elephants travel east to visit the president.

Words with the letter "T"

"T" Pronunciation Sentences

19. Twenty bats went to the royal court last Thursday, bought a bright light pot, and talked to Janet.

20. Tara took Elliott, the cat, to the vet because his tummy was truly terrible.

Where learning language online is fun!

Learning About the Sounds Letters Make!

Words with the letters "TH"

Learning About the Sounds Letters Make!

Where learning language online is fun!

Learning About the Sounds Letters Make!

Words with the letters "TH"

Words Starting with "TH"

Thacher, Thailand, Thanos Thelma, Theodore, Thor, than, thank, that, the, theater, their, them, theme, theory, therapy, there, thermometer, thick, thicken, thicker, thief, thieves, thimble, thin, thing, thinker, thinner, third, thirsty, this, thorn, thought, thought, thousand, thrash, threat, three, threw, thrifty, thriller, thrive, throat, throne, through, throughout, thumb, thump, thunder, thunderstorms

Words with "TH"

Agatha, Anthony, Arthur, Bertha, Kathleen, Othello, Timothy, another, asthma, athlete, author, bathtub, brother, clothes, earthy, either, empathy, father, feather, frothy, gather, lather, lethal, lithium, loathe, method, monthly, mother, mythical, nothing, other, pathway, python, rather, rethink, rhythm, slither, soothe, thread, weather, whether, wither, within, without, worthy

Words ending with "TH"

Beth, Kathleen, Keith, Lilith, Meredith, Ruth, Seth, beneath, bigmouth, birth, breath, cloth, death, earth, eighth, fifth, fourth, growth, gunsmith, health, length, locksmith, mammoth, math, month, moth, mouth, myth, ninth, north, path, sixth, sloth, smooth, south, strength, teeth, tenth, tollbooth, tooth, truth, truth, warmth, wealth, with, worth

Learning About the Sounds Letters Make!

Words with the letters "TH"

"TH" Pronunciation Sentences

1. The thumb thinks it should do a thumbs up and not a thumbs down.

2. The theory that the thief threw the thorns is thrilling but a myth.

3. Three thieves were thirsty, so they went south through the thick forest to the river.

4. The thirsty sloths thought three cups of water would make them thin and grow feathers.

5. My throat had thick thorns throughout the whole thing. I need something to soothe it.

6. Arthur thought a bathtub with thickened oatmeal would soothe his three sloths.

7. This big thief threw three thin volleyballs at Timothy.

8. The thunderstorm was the third thunderstorm the thirteen thieves thought of before thousands of thin toothpicks fell.

9. The third row is the best for the warmth of the warm weather.

10. My throat hurts, so I think my mother needs to get a thermometer.

11. Beth threw that thing with thick thorns through the thunderstorm because she thought there was a thief.

Where learning language online is fun!

Learning About the Sounds Letters Make!

Words with the letters "TH"

"TH" Pronunciation Sentences

12. The thick tiger had a mother and brother who loved to sit on the throne.

13. The traveler went to the theater, and there was a group of thieves.

14. Thanks to the eager thinker, Theodore threw the lethal rhythm to Anthony.

15. Arthur threw a thrilling party at the theater with yummy appetizers.

16. Agatha invited her sister, brother, the tired moth, and thirty thoughtful tigers to the theater.

17. Together, Arthur and his brother Roger made thermometers for the tenth time for the other author.

18. The path thumped with thunder and rhythm, and Thelma thrived to the thunderous beat.

19. Arthur, the author of the book "Theory of Rethinking a Thrifty Throne," thought thousands of fans would gather to hear his soothing words.

20. Beth was worth 100 thousand dollars that her mother and father stole from thirty thieves in the north.

Where learning language online is fun!

Learning About the Sounds Letters Make!

Where learning language online is fun!

Learning About the Sounds Letters Make!

Words with the letter "V"

Where learning language online is fun!

Learning About the Sounds Letters Make!

Learning About the Sounds Letters Make!

Words with the letter "V"

Words Starting with "V"

Venessa, Vicky, Viking, Vince, Virgil, Vitoria, Vivian, vacancy, vacation, vaccine, vacuum, valid, valley, van, vanilla, vanish, vapor, vase, veal, vegan, vegetable, vehicle, vent, venue, verb, verbal, versa, very, vest, vet, vibe, vibrant, vice, victim, video, view, vine, violet, violin, viper, vision, vision, visit, vitamin, vivid, voice, void, volcano, volleyball, volume, vomit, vote, vow

Words with "V"

Alvin, Ava, Calvin, Evelyn, Levi, Octavia, Savannah, Xavier, above, achieve, advice, alive, arrival, ave, avoid, brave, bravo, cave, covered, diva, dive, divided, division, envy, eve, even, event, every, evil, favorite, fever, five, flavor, give, glove, groove, heaven, hive, invitation, invite, ivy, knives, lava, level, love, movie, novel, olive, oval, oven, over, river seven, stove, twelve, wave, wolves

Words ending with "V"

Aviv, Lev, Liv, ganev improv, isogriv, leitmotiv, moshav, shiv

Where learning language online is fun!

Learning About the Sounds Letters Make!

Words with the letter "V"

"V" Pronunciation Sentences

1. The value of the van vase with vines is worthless!

2. The vicious Vikings were very weird and very worried about volleyball.

3. That diver divided that tart very slowly.

4. Vince the Viking thought volleyball was weird, but Vince the Viking was a very weird, thin, wacky whale.

5. Vince played the violin on vacation with a Viking.

6. There was a vanilla volcano that had vipers in diapers.

7. Vince divided the event between the Viking and the vegetable.

8. The event Vince was invited to had vipers, volcanoes, and sweet treats.

9. Vikings vacation with vanilla sweets on a very divided island.

10. Vince played volleyball with Vikings, Victor, Venus, and a violin.

11. A vegetable volcano violently vanished into the valley with a voice whispering, "Van, video, divided, victory, and vanilla vacuum."

12. Victor vomited after dividing the vanilla volcano cake at the event he was invited to with Victoria.

Learning About the Sounds Letters Make!

Words with the letter "V"

"V" Pronunciation Sentences

13. Vince, Victor, Victoria, and Vicky went on vacation with their violins. An event with five sweaty vultures wanted a vanilla volcano cake that Victoria had at her event.

14. Vice President Victoria saw visitors on vacation who listened to violins and ate vast amounts of vegan vanilla tarts.

15. Vicky saw Victoria violently vomit after Victor gave Vicky vegan vanilla tarts at Vince's volcano event.

16. Calvin went diving with Evelyn.

17. The viper vanished after a violent river flooded the valley.

18. Vivian ate vibrant vegetables covered in olive oil. She avoided the veal because Vivian is a vegan.

19. The cave had twelve evil wolves who all ate their vitamins, read novels, and loved video games.

20. The Viking visited Levi, who invited him over to race vehicles in the valley.

21. Octavia was very livid that Xavier covered her favorite gloves with knives and lava.

Where learning language online is fun!

Learning About the Sounds Letters Make!

Where learning language online is fun!

Learning About the Sounds Letters Make!

Words with the letter "W"

Where learning language online is fun!

Learning About the Sounds Letters Make!

Learning About the Sounds Letters Make!

Words with the letter "W"

Words Starting with "W"

Walter, Washington, Wendy, Whitney, William, Winnie, Winston, Wyatt, wag, wagon, wail, waist, waiter, waitress, wake, walk, wall, walnut, walrus, warm, warn, was, wash, waste, watch, water, waves, weather, web, week, weekday, weekend, went, were, west, wet, whale, what, wheel, whether, while, whine, white, who, wig, wiggle, willow, window, winter, witch, without, wizard, woman, wood, workout, worry, would, wow, wrist, write

Words with "W"

Darwin, Dewey, Dwight, Lewis, Shawna, Steward, await, awake, away, awhile, awkward, beware, bowl, bowler, brown, browse, clown, cowboy, crawl, crowd, dawn, down, drawer, eyewear, flower, freeway, gown, grown, hallway, hawk, jewel, known, lawn, lawyer, news, owl, powder, power, reward, runway, shower, subway, swan, sway, sweat, sweep, sweet, swim, swing, towel, tower, town, twelve, twice, twin, viewer

Words ending with "W"

Andrew, Drew, Harlow, Matthew, Willow, airshow, allow, anyhow, arrow, blow, bow, brew, burrow, cashew chew, chow, cow, dew, draw, elbow, few, flow, follow, hollow, jaw, jigsaw, law, marshmallow, meow, moonbow, nephew, outlaw, overshadow, paw, pillow, rainbow, saw, screw, shadow, snow, snow, stew, straw, threw, tomorrow, view, wheelbarrow, window, yellow

Where learning language online is fun!

Learning About the Sounds Letters Make!

Words with the letter "W"

"W" Pronunciation Sentences

1. Will Walter the Whale write with white ink to Wanda Walrus?

2. Wally wished for twelve sweet treats with a white clown.

3. What about that whale? Most whales went east last week! Mr. Whale will follow a cowboy and swim to meet his crowd.

4. William was worried Wendy would allow the witch to whine on the way west to Washington.

5. Would Whitney be watching the white snow in the woods when winter comes?

6. Would the white whale write a letter while warming watermelons?

7. Wendy went to meet Mr. Dewey, who was wearing a cowboy hat and wig.

8. Cow whined about his walnuts when he wanted twelve wedding cakes.

9. Wendy walked west on Westwood Street and saw a waitress washing a walrus with water.

10. Darwin hurt his wrist and waist while working out with a cow and a wizard.

11. Last weekend, my nephew went into the woods to find a weeping willow tree but found a subway with yellow flowers.

Learning About the Sounds Letters Make!

Words with the letter "W"

"W" Pronunciation Sentences

12. Winston had two pillow fights on a wet web with twelve walruses.

13. Drew wore a wig while a witch was riding a wagon looking for him in the wacky woods.

14. Winnie walked in the winter snow with a swan, a clown, and a wet cow.

15. The brown dog wagged his wet tail while swimming with whales and twenty walruses on a warm day.

16. The outlaw cowboy was aware of the wicked warm weather next week.

17. Wyatt woke up during the week at twelve o'clock and walked with Walter and Winnie to visit the wizard.

18. Willow saw a powerful magical jewel that would allow her to witness a wall.

19. "Wow," said the swan as she wiggled to the waves with Winston, the cow, and Dewey, the clown.

20. Whitney was a witch who whined about the winter weather because she walked without a winter sweater.

Learning About the Sounds Letters Make!

Where learning language online is fun!

Learning About the Sounds Letters Make!

Don't forget to check out our other books, **Daily Vocabulary Worksheets Volume 1 and 2 & Daily Vocabulary Flashcards Volume 1 and 2.**

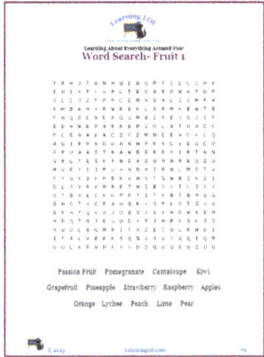

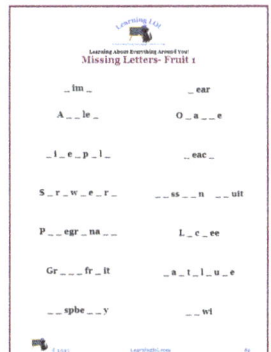

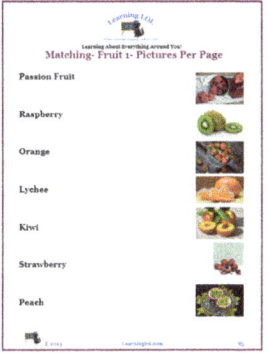

Where learning language online is fun!

Learning About the Sounds Letters Make!

www.ingramcontent.com/pod-product-compliance
Lightning Source LLC
Chambersburg PA
CBHW040512150626
46551CB00030B/2529